Noor upon Noor

Collection of Muslim Quotes.

Written by s.hukr

Noor upon Noor

Salam.

I hope you find peace, wisdom and love through these words. I hope this book inspires you to love yourself, educate yourself and become a better Muslim.

May Allah guide you towards that which is best while making your Dunya and your Deen easy for you.

If there is a word that you do not understand, simply search the definition of the word on Google.com.

e.g. "Define [word]"

fajrnoor.com.au

Noor upon Noor

You must first become knowledgeable
then you must become wise.

For when you have wisdom, you don't
have doubts. You don't have insecurities.

You know exactly what is what, even if
the whole world says something else.

s.hukr

Noor upon Noor

I see our men struggle with salah and
I see our women struggle with hijab.
I see our parents struggle with marriage
and our children struggle with mental health.

We struggle with basic things because
we live our life not according to Islam
but according to cultural & social norms.

s.hukr

Noor upon Noor

Let me remind you by saying that there is no such thing as feminism in Islam. Allah perfected our religion 1400 years ago.

Women were given their rights long before feminism was ever introduced to this world.

s.hukr

Noor upon Noor

I don't know about you, but I would rather
have Noor on my face than have money on
the table.

I would rather be in love, have divine
knowledge and be close to my lord than have
the temporary luxuries of this world.

This world is meaningless. It is a temporary. It
is a place of problems, trials, tribulations. It is
not my Paradise, and it will never be.

s.hukr

Noor upon Noor

People make dua and expect
things to fall from the sky.

That is not how you make dua.
That is not how you worship Allah.

s.hukr

Noor upon Noor

This world was not made for you and me.
We don't belong here; we will never fit in
and call this place our home.

As soon as the dust settles and we become
comfortable, a fire erupts from places we least
expect it and we are reminded that the peace
of this world is temporary.

s.hukr

Noor upon Noor

Did you find Laylatul Qadr?
Yes, I found Noor upon Noor.

s.hukr

Noor upon Noor

"Iqra!"

The first word revealed by Allah.

"Read" does not mean recite.
Allah didn't say recite, he said "Read".

Read means to comprehend and understand.

To understand we must use the intellect Allah
gave us. Don't read God's words blindly,
understand them and live by them.

s.hukr

Hijab is not only a headscarf that women must wear. It is the practice of Haya and Haya is the co-partner of Iman.

s.hukr

"Indeed, Haya and Iman are Companions. When one of them is lifted, the other leaves as well." – Baihaqi

Hijab of the Tongue:

You have duty to protect your tongue
from foul words, gossiping and lies.

Everything you speak about,
should be with Haya.

The way you speak about people should not
be sexualised, that is not respect. Do not make
jokes that hurt people, that is not humour.

Do not lie to satisfy people, that is not Islam.
Protect your tongue against harming others.

s.hukr

Hijab of the Eyes:

By staring at anything inappropriate, your eyes commit Zina. There is a reason why as Muslims we lower our gaze.

It is so we can protect our soul from its lustful desires and from sin. Be aware that Allah sees everything that you see, so lower your gaze.

s.hukr

Hijab of the Hands:

Do not allow your hands to do injustice to others or to yourself. Do not steal what is not yours. Do not assault an innocent person. Do not allow anyone to be harassed in front of you. Do not smuggle drugs, do not do them. Do not smoke sheesha, cigarettes or vapes.

They aren't good for your soul, nor will they help you on Yaumul Qiyamah. Allah is always watching you... remember that.

s.hukr

My age does not describe me.

You can have a 30-year-old who is immature
and childish, or you can have a 15 year old
who knows exactly what he is doing and in
complete control of his emotions
and way of life.

Age doesn't mean much, character does.

Age is just a measure of how long you have
lived but not how much you have learned,
experienced and endured life.

s.hukr

Noor upon Noor

We all go through hardship, but some of us are grateful, we have Sabr even when we have the right to complain.

We learn lessons, we subconsciously grow into the best version of ourselves. Because we know someone else has it worse than us.

We feel Alhamdulilah. We are thankful and grateful for even the trials and tests that we endure.

I think this is the attitude and mindset you need to be successful.

s.hukr

Hand in Marriage.

There is a way to ask someone's hand in marriage.

No, we do not flirt and play with people's hearts in the name of love and then think about marriage. We do not spend time with the opposite gender aimlessly.

This ummah is built on respect and dignity. We show this respect by seeking the approval of one's family. There is nothing wrong for a woman to propose and there is nothing wrong to reject a proposal as long as it is within the guidelines of Islam.

Race, age, height, hijab status and job title doesn't really matter. Prioritise their deen, their character, their manners, their ability to perform as a future mother/father.

If there is someone whom you like, always seek the counsel of someone because love often makes us blind. Then tell your family and their family. Meet each other under supervision of a mahram and if it's meant to be, Alhamdulillah and if not Alhamdulillah.

Our society needs to make marriage easy because it is the building block of society.

s.hukr

Noor upon Noor

Islam has made it clear that forced marriages
are forbidden.

That education is compulsory for every
Muslim regardless of gender.

Women in Islam are given the right to work,
to trade and earn such that her earning are her
own and that it is the duty of the Muslim man
to provide all the necessities for his family.

s.hukr

I don't like fan girls.

I don't mind people that show me love for the sake of Allah, but I don't like the idea that people love me more than they should.

Such people will compromise their Haya, create unrealistic fantasies in their head and become emotional for the sake of creation.

I suggest you stop being a "fan girl", a seeker of attention and temporary love. It always ends in heartbreak.

I recommend that you fill the void in your life with the love of Islam, understand your true purpose of being a Muslimah, live like a Queen should.

s.hukr

Noor upon Noor

If your way of dawah is pushing
people away from Islam.

Then you are the problem.

Not Islam.

s.hukr

Facilitating Haram is Haram.

As Muslims we do not support haram things especially when it can be avoided, and we do not facilitate haram, we discourage it without being judgemental.

This means that we do not work for a place that sells alcohol, pork or forbidden good/services such as Riba or an insurance company etc.

We do not support immodest fashion brands that promote nakedness. We do not support people who gossip, curse or disrespect someone in front of you.

We do not help friends get into a haram relationship or support an existing relationship of such nation. We do not support people or places that go against the teachings of Islam.

We don't judge them either,
we just keep our distance.

s.hukr

Noor upon Noor

My Dear Sister,

There is difference between being
beautiful and being seductive.

Being beautiful isn't a sin but
being sexually arousing in
public is a sin.

s.hukr

Noor upon Noor

Don't speak about something
you don't know.

It's okay to say, 'I don't know'
or 'I lack the knowledge to
talk about this'.

s.hukr

Noor upon Noor

The closer you get to Allah the more you
will find your world revolving around Islam.

The way you speak, your dress code,
your morals, the way you think,
even the way you eat will align with Islam.

To some Islam is just a religion, but it is so
much more than just a religion, it is perfect
vision of life.

It is a guidebook on how to live life to the
fullest. It is a just system of laws, regulations,
standards and ideas that are far superior then
the democracies of this world.

Its education is more beneficial than
universities that take away your money,
your peace and your passion.

Islam is beautiful, I hope more people study
the beauty of it and take time learning about it.

s.hukr

Noor upon Noor

"Verily with hardship comes ease."

Don't get lost in your pain that you
forgot about the cure that is promised.

Believing the cure will come
is half the medicine.

s.hukr

Noor upon Noor

When you find yourself commuting to work
or school, waiting for a long line or waiting for
Salah to begin at the mosque, in those
precious moments remember Allah.

Do Dhikr.

Remind your soul the reality of your existence.
The purpose of your life. Because at any
moment you can taste death. At any moment
Allah can take away your blessings, just
because you forgot about Him.

Remember Allah and He will remember you
and if you don't remember Him, He might
take away your blessings, so you may
remember him again.

s.hukr

Noor upon Noor

I could never imagine cheating on anyone.
It's the type of mistake and wrongdoing
I couldn't live with.

Knowing that you destroyed someone's
trust is bad but destroying someone's
perspective on love is a crime.

s.hukr

Noor upon Noor

I've always told people to respect their parents and to be kind to them. But some parents need a reminder that when they fail in their duty as parents, they will meet consequences.

Parents who love too much or love too little. Will end up neglecting their children and will often meet their consequences later in life.

Allah raised the status of parents in Islam but that doesn't mean you neglect your duty upon your children.

Children also have rights in Islam. If you neglect them you will face consequences.

s.hukr

Noor upon Noor

When I see this sad generation.

I don't blame them.
I look at their parents first.

Are they raising them with
culture or religion or both?

s.hukr

Noor upon Noor

Social media is a place full of lies because the majority of us only show a certain side of life.

Mostly the good, pretty, and perfect side. Completely hiding the pain, struggles and imperfections we go through.

I dislike how everything is so driven towards a fake and manipulated reality.

Girls with filters and excessive makeup so they always look picture perfect. Guys with perfect hair style and ripped figures, I think you get the idea.

Even on Instagram, your feed is catered towards your likes, not your dislikes. They feed you content that just stimulates your dopamine levels.

So you spend more time comparing yourself to a fake perception of reality.

s.hukr

Noor upon Noor

Reflect daily.

Bring closure to your day through 10 minutes of reflection.

Asks yourself:

"Did I pray all my Salah? "

"What went well, what didn't?"

"What needs improvement?"

"What's stopping me from improving?"

"Am I being the best I can be?"

"If death came tomorrow, would I be ready?"

"Do I understand my purpose in life?*

* add more self-reflecting questions *

s.hukr

Noor upon Noor

You must pray 5 times.
Because you are Muslim.

Image death came tomorrow.
And you didn't pray.
What a nightmare.

You would be lowered into your
grave being a non-Muslim.

s.hukr

Noor upon Noor

Some people need a mute button.

Speak only when you feel that your words are better than your silence because hell is filled with people who couldn't control their tongues.

Everything you say is written by angels on your shoulders, do not allow your tongue to be the reason why you suffer in the hereafter.

s.hukr

Noor upon Noor

I actually hate culture.

In some cultures, it's rude to come early.
In some cultures, it's okay to open a door
without knocking. In some cultures, people
have to fight to pay the dinner bill. In some
cultures, yelling is normal and being quiet is
seen as being shy.

In some cultures, men don't cook or clean,
they just work and make money. In some
cultures, husband and white do 50/5 split. In
some cultures, haram is normalised and halal is
considered extreme religious behaviour.

But I love Islam.

It's such a peaceful and balanced way of living.
It is according to Allah's instructions, what He
has ordained for us. It is very beautiful, simple
and easy. That's why I strive for.

But unfortunately, more than half the Muslim
population follows culture not Islam.

s.hukr

Noor upon Noor

Some people are too desperate. They don't know how to let things go. Why do we run after people, money and temporary things? I guess, it's to fulfil a desire, but at what cost?

It's okay to pursue our desires & dreams but only if they are halal and the means in which we pursue them is morally and ethically acceptable in Islam.

It is okay to have the desire to be wealthy, but do not allow the desire to control you. If you become wealthy by haram activities, then you become a sinner.

Similarly, it is okay to have the desire to be beautiful, but if you perform unnecessary and extensive beauty treatments that go against the teachings of Islam, then you become a sinner.

You are the master of your soul, but if you let the devil inside, he will become your master and you become the devil's slave.

s.hukr

Noor upon Noor

I've noticed that women in western societies are treated differently than in the east.

Both cater to extremes that I don't like. Some are too liberated thus losing their value and others are too conservative that their basic rights are stripped.

I don't like either because they aren't the way of Islam. Islam is balanced, in the middle.

s.hukr

Noor upon Noor

Sister,

Your purpose isn't to dress to impress the public and then have the audacity to say men don't lower their gaze.

We all know Allah created men weak in this regard, but you aren't helping by being a makeup clown.

You need a better definition for beauty, because fake lashes, fake nails, caked up faces and other haram beauty treatments are not sources of real beauty.

s.hukr

Noor upon Noor

Sis, I know the way you look at him. What are you scared off, that he will say yes?

There's nothing wrong if your intentions are pure. Tell your father or tell your brother, tell someone so you may learn more about him.

Talk to him, ask him a few questions, it's not what he says but how he says it. Don't look at his wealth, look at his character, is he hardworking, honest and a man of Allah?

Make Dua and if Allah puts love of this man inside you then what are you waiting for? Thank Allah for the blessings he sent your way and then tell your family. Go complete half your Deen.

Do not give up so easily especially when you are doing nothing wrong in the eyes of God.

s.hukr

Noor upon Noor

Our children are our future. If you neglect them, you neglect your future.

If you spoil and love them too much, you're actually doing them harm in the long term. And if you are too harsh and strict with them, they will want to distance themselves from you.

As a parent, we must strike a balance, a balance that was shown to us by the Prophet ﷺ and his companions.

We must raise our children with the teachings of Islam. Islam is perfect by design; you must accept that. It was created by Allah and the messenger of Allah showed us how to implement it.

I pray that we raise a strong future for this ummah.

s.hukr

Noor upon Noor

Islam is so beautiful, that if you make Dua for someone, the angels make Dua for you.

So honour the guests of your heart.

s.hukr

Noor upon Noor

I hope one day I can leave this world
knowing that I raised a strong little
king and a brilliant young queen.

s.hukr

Noor upon Noor

Life on earth is like a handshake between
the hand of love and the hand of hate.

s.hukr

Some examples of good conduct and love between The Prophet ﷺ and his wives.

1. He would never hit his wives.
2. He would let things slide by not picking/addressing every little mistake.
3. He would play and joke around with them.
4. He would help them whenever they required help.
5. He would give them nicknames e.g. He used to call Aa'isha (ra) 'O Aa'ish' or 'Humayra' which signifies something that is small and red.
6. He would drink from the exact same part of the vessel from where his wife would drink from.
7. He would spend on them.
8. He would do things on their behalf even after their death like when he sacrificed an animal and gave some of the meat to Khadija's (ra) friends.
9. When A'a'isha (ra) was on her menstrual cycle, he would lean against her and recite Quran while they both rested.

s.hukr

Noor upon Noor

In Islam,

a Mahram is a member of one's family with
whom marriage would be considered haram;
from whom concealment of the body with
hijab, is not obligatory; and with whom, if he
is an adult male, she may be escorted during a
journey, although an escort may not be
obligatory.

s.hukr

44

What is Mahr?

In Islam, Mahr is compulsory.

It is a form of gift that is given by the groom to the bride at the time of Marriage.

While Mahr is often money, it can also be anything agreed upon by the bride such as jewellery, home goods, hajj or even a Quran.

It is a gift that is agreed upon by both parties. It shouldn't be too much nor too low but a reasonable amount according to one's social economic status.

s.hukr

Islam is about balance not about extremes, you should specify a low Mahr for Barakat, as the Prophet ﷺ said: "The most blessed Nikah is the one with least expenses." – Bayhaqi

Noor upon Noor

I think people don't know how to love.
Especially men. Nobody teaches us how
to love properly.

Some of us love our parents and neglect our
wives, some of us love our children and
neglect our parents. Some of us love material
things and neglect our hereafter and some of
us love 'Deen' and neglect our Dunya.

Balance is key and is achieved when Allah is in
the centre of the heart. We must live our life
according to the Quran and Islam. We must
learn how to distribute our love equally
amongst each aspect of our life. Not pouring
too much nor pouring too little but just the
right amount.

There is blessing when we follow
the ways of the Prophet ﷺ.

s.hukr

Noor upon Noor

My love, once I find you, I will treasure you
like a gem from the heavens because you are
God's greatest gift to me.

I will move mountains for you, bring you
peace after every hardship and comfort you to
the best of my ability but never allow your
ego to hinder my connection with God.

s.hukr

Please stop normalising marriage amongst cousins. Amongst your own race and your own people.

I know that it is halal but there are almost 2 billion Muslims today and this ummah needs to be united.

I think Marriage is one of the ways we can create powerful bonds. The bond of marriage can unite two different families, two different bloodlines, two different countries and two different cultures.

Let us create bonds between this ummah, stop living in your toxic cultured mindset. There is nothing wrong to marry another Muslim from a different country, culture, or family.

Actually, the Prophet did it.
So why can't you?

s.hukr

Noor upon Noor

I hope we can unite and inspire enough
change to see the children of Palestine,
Afghanistan, Uyghurs and all Muslim
nations to wake up to peace
and prosperity.

For that to happen, we must unite
under the ways of Islam.

We must let go of our ego, our
culture and our comfort zone.

s.hukr

Noor upon Noor

May Allah unite this ummah as strong as the
bonds between atoms, grant us faith stronger
than mountains and place in our land's
protection from injustice and cruelty.

I pray this ummah comes to the
realisation that we must get up
and do what needs to be done.

s.hukr

Noor upon Noor

I feel that Muslim women aren't
beautiful as they once were.

No, I'm not talking about everyone but a
growing majority. I'm not talking about
outward beauty, that isn't as important
as the beauty within.

There used to be an aura glowing within
them and when you saw a glimpse
of their face, you would see Noor.

I barely see it these days.

s.hukr

Noor upon Noor

You are already physically beautiful but it's the
beauty of the soul that excites another soul.

s.hukr

Noor upon Noor

I hear many girls and guys
complain about one another.

Girls complain about how there
aren't any good guys and guys
complain about the same reality.

Stop focusing on the other gender.

Focus on yourself. Because I bet half
of you struggle with the simple things
in Islam, like praying on time.

Instead of complaining and pointing out the
flaws in one another, focus on yourself so
much, in terms of personality and character,
and then watch how you attract people like a
magnet.

"Verily, Good women are for good men and
good men are for good women".

s.hukr

Noor upon Noor

Brother,

She isn't looking for riches,
beauty or poetry. She is looking
to be understood, respected and loved.

Respect is how you attract her, understanding
her will give her security and love will make
her yours forever.

Why are men of this generation
so dumb and selfish?

s.hukr

Noor upon Noor

Teach your children common sense because apparently, they don't teach that anymore.

Teach them kindness, love and tell them about the delights of Paradise. So they make that their goal in life and not money, fame or worldly success.

s.hukr

Only guys will understand this:

Late night driving, windows down, no music,
no friends, alone, silently listening to the wind.

Moments of Peace. Clarity. And Wisdom.

s.hukr

Noor upon Noor

Allah made the Quran for us to read, to read
with understanding and comprehension.

So tell me why is it on the
bookshelf collecting dust?

s.hukr

Noor upon Noor

This world is tiring.
I look forward to the day of escape.
My unappreciated soul needs rest.

s.hukr

Ghayrah - غَيْرَة

In Islam we have a concept of Ghayrah. Ghayrah is an Arabic word which loosely translates to protective jealously.

I find it strange when I see Men who are not even embarrassed when their wives, sisters and womenfolk are all dressed up, ready to attract the attention of other men. They don't care if another man mingles with their womenfolk.

Let me remind you, that we follow Islam. And all Muslim men should have a collective sense of protectiveness for Muslim women as Allah says in the Quran: "The Men are the protectors and maintainers of women…" (Quran 4:34).

It is a major sin for a Muslim Man to not have Ghayrah. Ghayrah is a good type of jealousy, it is a natural inbuilt feeling Allah has given men and women. I personally think it is more important for men to have this feeling of jealously.

But both Muslim men and women must protect and guard one another from indecency, we should have this uneasiness in our hearts of Ghayrah, because not having it, leads to major sins.

s.hukr

Noor upon Noor

Honestly, life is full of wonders;
God makes the unthinkable happen.

We plan something but Allah has
something better planed for us.

So always trust him with your fate.
Just never give up trying your best.

s.hukr

Noor upon Noor

Sometimes I get messages from complete strangers that I've never met. Paragraphs telling me how I've changed their life.

They sharing their story with me and it genuinely brings me a joy. I find it amazing how a few words on a piece of paper can inspire people towards success.

Towards happiness. Towards self-change.

I don't believe the miracle comes from me, rather it is always Allah who guides us, and this is his miracle.

My advice would be to become people who inspire goodness, don't force religion, display in a such a beautiful manner within yourself that people would love to be your friend.

Your character becomes the reason Noor shines on your face and attracts people closer to their lord.

s.hukr

Noor upon Noor

I witness brothers wear short shorts,
ripped jeans and clothing that would be
inappropriate for Salah?

The same is true for the sisters. Why is
there an opportunity given for people to
commit Zina of the eyes?

If your clothing isn't adequate for your 5
daily prayers then you need to change
your wardrobe immediately.

s.hukr

"Modest Fashion" is a term that gets used a lot but it's not always modest, don't let the devil trick you.

What is modest clothing?

Modest clothing means a piece of clothing that covers in such a way that it does not expose your adornments. It covers and does not reveal your features in way that would seduce the opposite gender.

s.hukr

Noor upon Noor

I find it crazy how easily you can influence people, yani if I say, 'Girls who wear abayas are cute', a group of girls are now more likely to consider wearing it.

Yes, we should influence people in a positive manner, but my opinions shouldn't have more weight in your life than Islam or any other person for that matter.

Islam should always have more priority in your life than anyone's opinion unless the other persons opinion completely aligns with Islam.

s.hukr

Noor upon Noor

Idk who needs to hear this but you gotta stop smoking shesha, like are you waiting for the doctors to discover a new disease that you might have? or do you want your heart clouded by whims of Dunya and destined for hell?

I really dislike seeing Muslims at shesha lounges or clubs. Brother go to the mosque instead, visit the house of Allah. Let go of the places where sin is common. I don't wanna see you in hell, begging for a second chance.

s.hukr

Noor upon Noor

I avoid women. I avoid an easy life.
I avoid things that make me weak.

I've noticed the further away
I stay away from pleasure and comfort.
The strong I become.

s.hukr

Noor upon Noor

Idk why Muslims have such big luxurious
weddings, there is absolutely no Barakat, no
humbleness, no modesty, no sense of Sunnah.

They spend all this money and effort telling
people about their marriage that just began
without any guarantee that it will not end in a
divorce. May Allah guide you.

I would rather invest in my marriage or go on
a honeymoon with my wife than have a
luxurious wedding with people who I barely
know.

s.hukr

Noor upon Noor

I used to think all Muslims were the same.

They would all have the same set of beliefs,
ideals and morals. Their opinions and mindset
would align with the Quran.

However, I was very wrong.

I found out that Muslims forgot how to read
the Quran. They changed read to recite,
sunnah to optional, made halal difficult and
haram easy.

Then they started to differentiate themselves
into different categories. Liberal or traditional,
Shia or Sunni. Moderate or practicing,
upper and lower class etc.

Why can't we have people with a balanced
mindset. Neither east or west, nor up or down,
but centred. Why can't every Muslim pick up
the Quran and start reading until they
understand what Allah wants them to do?

s.hukr

Do sects exist in Islam?

No. Islam is not made up of sects.

Yes, some people have divided our religion into different "sects", but Islam is one religion perfected by Allah through the messenger of Allah, as mentioned in the Quran:

"This day have I perfected your religion for you, completed My favour upon you, and have chosen for you Islam as your religion." 5:3

We are one ummah united under God's book. We follow the teachings of the Prophet ﷺ because Allah told us to in His book.

...

If people preach "Islam" that goes against the teachings of Quran and Sunnah, then they are answerable and held accountable by Allah.

"And if Allah had willed, He could have made you [of] one religion, but He causes to stray whom He wills and guides whom He wills. And you will surely be questioned about what you used to do." 16:93

"Indeed, those who have divided their religion and become sects - you, [O Muhammad], are not [associated] with them in anything. Their affair is only [left] to Allah; then He will inform them about what they used to do." 6:159

s.hukr

Noor upon Noor

Having disagreements with others should
not be the reason why hate enters your heart.

Just because you disagree with someone
about something, shouldn't be the reason
why you abandon that friendship.

It's okay that you don't meet common
ground. It's not a reason to be rude, to
be selfish, to show ill character.

It should not be the reason why we push
people away. Learn to defuse a situation
with your excellent character. It's not your
job to make sure everyone you meet has
the same mindset as you.

Be open minded enough to let people
express themselves even if you believe
them to be wrong.

Remember, love is far more effective
than any sort of hate.

s.hukr

Noor upon Noor

Parents these days are not very
good at parenting. Trust me I know.

Too many young people share their
problems with me and 80% of those
problems occur within the house.

I'm not here to point fingers,
I'm here to share the reality.

s.hukr

Noor upon Noor

Our parents seem to follow their parents,
the culture and tradition that they were
subjected to as children. Which doesn't
work in today's world.

Especially culture and traditional values that
do not align with the ways of Islam. They
will never work in the long run. They will
become one of the reasons why children
have problems.

Instead, raise your children according to
Islamic values and principles. It's far
more easier and rewarding.

s.hukr

Noor upon Noor

A women's primary purpose is not to go
outside and get the bread for the house, it is
not her responsibility to earn like a man.
Rather a women's weakness is the Dunya.

Her primary purpose is to maintain and
establish her domain within her household.

She is the Queen of the palace so to speak.
Her duty is to her household, her husband,
and her children. She must meet those duties
with good regard and only then, can she
consider establishing herself outside the
household.

s.hukr

Noor upon Noor

You need to stop putting yourself down,
You need to learn to love yourself,
You need to educate yourself,
You need to read the Quran, learn the sunnah,
You need to improve and grow,
You need to be strong and smart,
You need to be sincere and loveable,
You need to forgive yourself and move on,
You need to glow up,
You need to give yourself time,
You need to be physically fit and mentally able,
You need to forbid evil and encourage good,
You need to be wise and humble,
You need to be a True Muslim.

Not for me, but for yourself because you
desire Jannah. I know you can do it because
Allah said so.

You will be questioned on Yaumil Qiyamah
about the time you spend in this Dunya.
So start preparing yourself.

s.hukr

Noor upon Noor

Oi Muslim!

Please stop telling people your star sign,
zodiac sign or whatever you call it.

It is Shirk.

Do you want to die a non-Muslim?

s.hukr

"OMG did I tell you about Sarah?"

Judging others and being judged has become a very common issue that troubles the hearts and disturbs the peace. You might have witnessed this in one way or the other.

As Muslims we have no right to make negative assumption of anyone and publicise it.

The clothes they wear, the way they make decisions, their good or bad deeds, whatever it maybe. It doesn't give you the right to think bad of that person or speak ill of them to others.

Islam commands us to intervene and stop the back biting that occurs in front of us. Islam teaches us to assume the best in people even when things may look differently, but that doesn't mean you turn a blind eye to an obvious crime.

...

Noor upon Noor

Only Allah has the right to judge us for He sees the unseen aspects of our lives. He knows what is in our hearts, what goes through our minds and the circumstances we go through.

But we also have a duty to guide others in a respectful and well-behaved manner. To encourage good in them not only with our tongues but more so with our actions.

Noor upon Noor

Pointing out someone's flaws in public space whether it be in real life or in the comment section does not entail proper Dawah.

There is a correct way of giving advice. Sometimes that means completing ignoring them.

s.hukr

"It's nOt HaRam, wHerE dOes iT SaY tHat iN tHe Quran?"

Please stop using this excuse, it makes you look stupid and arrogant. It doesn't have to be stated in the Quran specifically for it to be haram.

As Allah told us in the Quran, to the follow the teachings of the Prophet ﷺ in chapter 4 verse 59. Look it up yourself.

So if the Prophet of Allah said it is Haram, it is Haram.

s.hukr

Noor upon Noor

Let me ask you the following:

School and University prepares you for what?

To make money? To busy yourself in the pursuits of worldly matters? To enjoy the temporarily pleasures of life?

To buy material things in the hope that it fills the void in your soul? To have bread on the table?

Is that all this life means to us?

What kind of knowledge is that? What kind of lifestyle is that? Are we not Muslims who live our life according to the ways of Islam?

So why are we living the lifestyle of the non-Muslims?

s.hukr

Noor upon Noor

I witness Muslims nowadays celebrating Pagan
traditions. Pagan traditions like Birthdays,
gender reveals, new years and even Christmas.

They aren't really Muslims.
They are hypocrites.

They prioritise worldly
life over Islam.

s.hukr

Noor upon Noor

I've met a lot of people in my life, but I don't like most people I meet. I don't care how rich, pretty or intelligent you are. I don't care about your social status.

My heart likes the company of those who are conscious of Allah. Not the judgemental type or those with a skewed perception of reality but those who are gentle, kind and soft inside.

Their presence makes me feel blessed and happy, the way they think, the way they behave isn't like normal people,
its pure and prestige.

They are wise enough to be humble and strong enough to tell the truth, but never in such a manner that would hurt you.

I meet them once and I already know they are different from the rest. It's like I met a person from Paradise.

s.hukr

Noor upon Noor

Nowadays, I find people to be afraid
of themselves. They have forgotten the
duty that one owes to oneself.

The basic necessity.

The duty of self-love, self-respect
and self-learning.

s.hukr

Noor upon Noor

The light of Islam is coming.
The devil will be locked up.

The gates of Hell will be closed.
Heaven will be open again.

Blessing upon blessings will shower.
Good deeds will increase 10-fold.

The month of Quran.
Ramadan.

s.hukr

Noor upon Noor

I faced hardship early in life, it aged
my soul but beautified my heart.

God answered my wishes
I used to cry over.

Alhamdulilah.

s.hukr

Noor upon Noor

I'm constantly learning new things, exploring
new experiences, pushing my limits because
God didn't create me to be useless.

He made me to be the best of creation.

s.hukr

Noor upon Noor

If you're a Muslim and you start a
conversation with me by saying hey or hello.

I'm going to block you.

Say Assalamu alaykum or Salam,
it's more soothing to my soul.

s.hukr

Noor upon Noor

The teacher is always silent during
the test and every student has the
potential to get the highest mark.

Some just never try their absolute best.

s.hukr

Noor upon Noor

People are delusional.

They expect you to read their mind and give them exactly what they desire. I find them strange because they expect from the creation, not from the creator.

They misplace their trust and hope in people. Only to become hopeless, heartbroken, and depressed until they realise what they desire lies only with Allah and they should only seek it from Him.

s.hukr

Noor upon Noor

If you're getting almost everything
that you desire in this world without
much struggle.

Then you must ask yourself is Allah
giving me my reward in this life and
reserving my punishment in the
hereafter?

s.hukr

Noor upon Noor

Not everything is about you.

This world doesn't revolve around you.
You are not the centre of attention.
You are nothing but a sec of dust.

The more you crave attention the more
insignificant you become to me.

s.hukr

Noor upon Noor

It's funny how I notice Muslims buying from luxury brands. Temporary things that will not help in the hereafter.

They fall into this idea that if I buy from brands like LV, Gucci or Mercedes. They will be seen as successful, rich and beautiful.

But in reality, majority of them miss their 5 daily prayers, are insecure about how they look and financially dependent on others.

Isn't Salah our path to success?
Isn't Quran the way we beautify ourselves?
Isn't charity how we get richer in the eyes of Allah?

s.hukr

Noor upon Noor

If I ever get married, I'm gonna post pictures of the sky and act like nothing happened.

During the night, I'll wakeup and thank Allah for the blessings He bestowed upon me.

I'm not here to make others jealous, I'm not here to make people feel lonely. I'm not here to please creation or feel better about myself.

Because the evil eye is very real.

s.hukr

Noor upon Noor

Don't believe everything you hear.

Always do your due diligence.

s.hukr

Noor upon Noor

If you hear of my death, make Dua for me.

Ask Allah to forgive and pardon me for all my sins. Ask Him to have mercy on me and to make my grave a good resting place. Ask Him to grant me safe passage to Jannah.

It would be nice to see everyone in Jannah including you.

s.hukr

Noor upon Noor

The life is this Dunya starts to become boring
every time I start to read about Paradise.

s.hukr

Noor upon Noor

What is belief and what is disbelief?

What does it mean to believe in Allah?
What does it mean to believe in Islam?

Allah tells us in the Quran.

When we follow the ways of Islam,
our belief in Allah increases, we
become more blessed, educated,
righteous and more in control
of our self.

And when we don't follow Islam,
we allow disbelief to enter our hearts.
We stop seeking knowledge, we allow
our tongue to lie, backbit and do evil.

We allow disbelief to enter our hearts such
that we may describe ourself as a hypocrite.

s.hukr

Noor upon Noor

What is friendship?

A true friend is someone who understands your perspective. Someone whom you trust to share your personal matters.

A person who loves you enough to not support you when you are wrong but is always there when you need them.

No distance of time can separate you from them. They want what is best for you in accordance with Allah, not their own self-interest or your own self-interest.

They give you good advice and constantly remind you of Allah. They want to see you succeed in life.

s.hukr

Noor upon Noor

I hope you don't find what
you're looking for.

Rather, I wish that Allah grants
you whatever is best for you.

s.hukr

Noor upon Noor

Don't hold back compliments it could make someone's day, while you earn a good deed.

s.hukr

Noor upon Noor

I don't like this generation.

We fight over petty things,
over temporary things.

The men are half the problem
and the other half are the women.

Instead of complaining about
each other. Learn to understand
and appreciate each other.

s.hukr

Noor upon Noor

The scars on my body have healed, they
don't bother me. But the scars on my
heart are sawed with fine thread.

Sometimes people say things they
shouldn't and the thread breaks.

Pain overflows and tears start to flow.
So I carry myself back to Allah in the
hope that he may mend my heart again.

Be careful of your tongue.

s.hukr

Noor upon Noor

"You can't water the rose of a stubborn garden".

You can't force religion; you can't force
faith and you definitely can't force love.

s.hukr

Noor upon Noor

I don't like religious people.

They will push you away from Islam, make you feel bad for not practicing Islam and will embarrass and judge you in public.

But I love righteous people.

They pull you closer to Jannah without even making you realise it. They actually help to put you back on your deen in the most loving and compassionate way. Their moral compass starts to influence yours just with their presence.

They are like a magnet that pulls you closer towards real beauty, love and peace.

Those are the real Muslims that I love.

s.hukr

Noor upon Noor

The older you get the more you really want someone with Iman in their heart, a warm smile, arms that hug you into comfort and when you look at them, you are reminded of how blessed you are to be with them.

s.hukr

Noor upon Noor

People are funny. People tell me they need my books or they need a certain item for a certain occasion. However, they are confusing with what they need and what they want.

There are only a few things
people actually need in life:

Food, Water, Shelter, Air and
Clothing. That's about it.

Everything else is just desires.
Think about it.

Are you in control of
your desires or are you
a slave of your desires?

s.hukr

Noor upon Noor

Hijab makes you look confident, beautiful
and you feel like royalty. There are so many
benefits to the Hijab and I always admire
Queen energy.

I know this world makes it difficult to be
modest and to feel beautiful. But that's
part of the test of this Dunya.

Allah made Hijab compulsory.
There must be wisdom behind it.
The harder the Hijab is for you,
the greater the reward from Allah.

Maybe you're not ready, but at least put some
effort towards it by purchasing some Hijabs.
Trying them on, with time, I'm certain Allah
will make it easy for you.

Show Allah that you are willing to change your
entire wardrobe for His sake. You want to
enter Jannah, right?

So keep trying your best.
I pray Allah makes easy for you.

s.hukr

Noor upon Noor

Men need to understand that when a woman is stressed, she just wants to talk, and all you need to do is listen, not to offer solutions.

She just wants to be heard and understood even if she makes zero sense. She just wants attention from someone who cares about her.

s.hukr

Noor upon Noor

When you realise the power of words,
you'll start to say less and
choose your words carefully.

When you realise the power of thought,
you won't waste time overthinking.

When you realise the power of influence,
you won't surround yourself with just anyone.

s.hukr

Some people forgive but not with their whole heart. They forgive but then close their heart towards that person.

The poison of one's crime remains in their heart and fuels ill emotions towards the other.

If you really want to forgive, then do so with your whole heart. Forgive that person as if you forgotten their crime. Clean your heart of all anger and hate.

Because when Allah forgives us, He does not punish us, he doesn't remind us of our short comings, instead he wipes away our sin and replaces them with good deeds.

s.hukr

Noor upon Noor

Sometimes I make a simple mistake
just to see how people react and to
reveal the true nature of people.

Then accordingly, I distance myself
from the toxic ones and become
closer to the good ones.

s.hukr

Noor upon Noor

Muslims attacking Muslims.

My heart aches at how nasty
we become in a blink of an eye.

Perhaps this is another test
from Allah to see who is who.

s.hukr

Noor upon Noor

I don't think I'll ever fall in love with
this world. I've already seen the ugly
truth behind the fake curtains of
perfection.

I dream of Paradise.
I hope I'm allowed inside and
if I'm not, I pray someone's
Paradise isn't complete
without me.

s.hukr

Allah is so merciful, so loving and so just. That He sends down trials and tribulations in this life for the sins we have committed, to protect us from the punishment of the hereafter.

s.hukr

I heard Allah's Messenger as saying: There is nothing (in the form of trouble) that comes to a believer even if it is the pricking of a thorn that there is decreed for him by Allah good or his sins are obliterated. - Sahih Muslim 2572g

Noor upon Noor

Most men think in 1 dimension. Logic
Most women think in 1 dimension. Emotions.

To become a great person, you must live your
life in 3 dimensions. Consider logic, emotions,
and divinity.

Not allowing either one to take more control
than it should. You must maintain balance, so
you can maintain order and so you can achieve
greatness.

s.hukr

Noor upon Noor

If I were to thank Allah for a
thousand years, it would still
not be enough.

I hope these tears that come
from my heart, the ones that
are full of Gratitude are
heavy on the scales.

s.hukr

Noor upon Noor

An intelligent man doesn't concern
himself with the opinions of the sheep.

He knows that when you mess with a
pack of wolves, no sheep is safe.

s.hukr

Noor upon Noor

"Why is life so confusing?"

It's not. You never took time to
understand the book about life.

"Which book?"

The book written by Allah,
the one who created life.

s.hukr

Noor upon Noor

A man's shoulders were built for
responsibility. He works all his life
to fulfill that responsibility.

He is a giver, he gives from his wealth, his
time and his mind. He maintains the order of
his family, provides for his family and spends
on his family.

Not only his family but also he is responsible
for playing a part of his community.

Being a man is no easy task. But it becomes
extraordinarily difficult when his own family
becomes a burden on his shoulders.

The biggest burden a man can face is a wife
who doesn't obey, who doesn't listen, while
he has not done an ounce of injustice to her.

But has provided for her all necessities and
given her the best of his ability. Such women
are cursed by Allah.

s.hukr

Noor upon Noor

Why is everyone so selfish now?

I feel people don't take friendship seriously anymore. I feel that the reason we become friends with someone is not aligning with our faith.

People often become friends with you for a benefit or perhaps you seek friendship because you feel lonely even if that friendship is bad for you spiritually, mentally or physically.

I miss the good old days when friendship was based on the condition of one's soul. We used to make friends based on the aura of their soul.

We made bonds with people who we could help or provide mutual benefit, knowing that this person has a good heart, or this friendship may inspire goodness within the community.

s.hukr

Noor upon Noor

I know deep down your hurting. You try to control yourself but somehow tears fall down without you realising. You don't understand why it's hurting so much but it does.

Let those rivers fall, let your heart clean itself because it is about time you look inwards. You need to figure out what's wrong and reflect upon yourself, and if you still can't find peace, carry yourself to Allah. Verily, it is He who mends the heart.

s.hukr

Noor upon Noor

One of man's greatest joy is a reliable speedy horse. Even nowadays they measure it with horsepower.

But the horse that lies in his heart, has only one saddle. That is man's greatest joy. Not everyone gets to ride that horse.

s.hukr

Noor upon Noor

When you meet new people, pay close
attention to what they ask you and
how they ask you.

I find most people are not interested
in you, but in your temporary attributes,
like your wealth, your status, your beauty
and in your education. They are selfish,
they only focus on how you can help them.

They focus on stuff that doesn't matter,
stuff that doesn't describe the condition
of one's soul.

It's rare when I meet people, that they
aren't concerned about this life because
they have already fallen in love with the
idea of the next world.

s.hukr

Noor upon Noor

If you understand the laws of God and the fundamentals of Life. You will start to live life very differently to everyone else.

Because now you know what is right and what is wrong, you understand what is important and what is not. You know exactly what to do and what not to do.

You'll start to live life like a traveller on a journey.

s.hukr

Noor upon Noor

Be the person that hides sins and encourages good in others in such a way that it makes them smile and happy.

Be that person that has such high morals and ethics that it inspires others to fall in love with Islam.

It makes me sad how we fight amongst ourselves and let hatred enter our heart.

Where is your Mercy?
Where is your Love?
Where is your Compassion?

s.hukr

"Whoever conceals [the faults of] a Muslim, Allah will conceal [his faults] in this life and the Hereafter." - Muslim

Noor upon Noor

She showed me her beauty and expected
me to approach her, but I turned a blind
eye and ignored her.

She came back and said, "Am I not beautiful?"
so I said, "Yes, you are beautiful, but God
has reserved me for someone else, you are not
mine."

She walked away confused as if she never
faced rejection before. Pondering at how
she still had respect for a man who told
her "no".

I later found out that she had converted
to Islam. When they told me about her
story, they said, a faithful man reminded
her of God in such a way that she cried
all night until she found Islam.

s.hukr

Noor upon Noor

Apparently, 80% of single Muslims have someone they would like to marry but are too afraid from rejection.

I thought Muslims only fear Allah.

Why are we scared from something that is halal? Asking someone's hand in Marriage is the best way to complete half your Deen.

This is your sign to get married or to move forward with your life. Either commit to it or let it go.

Make a decision and quit wasting your time overthinking everything.

s.hukr

Noor upon Noor

I have no right to judge you, but Allah will definitely judge you. So you have a choice, either be a Muslim or don't be one. Simple.

Don't play this game of being a hypocrite. Don't play around in this world having a false label on your head that says "Muslim".

s.hukr

Noor upon Noor

You can dress attractively to your hearts content but only for your spouse.

You are not allowed to be immodest in-front of others.

You must be careful of your dress code as it has direct relationship with the respect you might receive.

But remember... do not be that human being that judges' others with a blink of an eye. For such people is a humiliating punishment from Allah.

s.hukr

7 Steps to help you face difficult situations:

1. Salah:

Make sure you stick to praying on time – 5 times a day. Never miss salah and do your best to pray each Salah with sincerity as if it's your last prayer in this world.

2. Read Quran:

Quran is so beautiful that no matter what difficulties you face you'll find solace in it. Read it carefully with understanding.

3. Make Dua:

The Dua for removing anxiety: "O Allah, I take refuge in You from anxiety and sorrow, weakness and laziness, miserliness and cowardice, the burden of debts and from being over powered by men." - Sahih al-Bukhari, 7/158

4. Give Sadaqah:

Give lots of charity, as much as you can, because it helps push away hardship. And if you can't give money, even kind words or a smile will do.

. . .

5. Set Goals and Have Vision:

Don't let Shaytan play with you and keep replaying the video of your hardship in your mind over and over again, move on! Set new goals, new projects, and remember you're with Allah, nothing should stop you!

6. Wake up Early:

Wake up before Fajr and work on your ideas and projects, or simply read Quran. Getting busy before daybreak is a definite way to move away from your hardship and overcome challenges. Get most of your ideas/work done in these early hours.

7. Hardship is Not Lost:

Remember, Allah will never forget the injustice and hardship you faced, so don't worry about seeking revenge or trying to get justice.

Keep knocking on God's door until He changes your fate. Not according to your best interest but according to whatever is best for your soul.

s.hukr

Noor upon Noor

Never hurt a heart full of love,
because if it breaks, that heartache
may turn into a curse that will follow
you to your grave.

s.hukr

Noor upon Noor

It depends how blessed or
cursed you want to be.

You already know that there are plenty
of things you could be doing to improve your
connection with Allah.

To improve the condition of
your heart, your body and soul.

However, your enemy, the Shaytans and his
whispers get to you. Therefore, stopping you
from reaching your true potential in life.

Allah doesn't burden us; Allah doesn't want
us to be miserable or depressed or cursed.

There are people who put 1% into self-
improvement and others who put in 110%.

It's all on you and how desperately you
want to change yourself.

s.hukr

Noor upon Noor

I just wanna build my empire now and help people as best as I can. Leave this world better than how I found it.

s.hukr

Noor upon Noor

We all like to believe that Allah would allow us into his Paradise. That He will show us mercy and forgiveness. And Yes, He is the most merciful and forgiving.

But some of us will never smell the fragrance of Jannah, some of us do not deserve Jannah, because we simply do not follow Islam.

We are insincere with Allah.
So prepare for His Wrath.

s.hukr

Noor upon Noor

Whenever life has tested me with something
and I passed the test, Allah has always
rewarded me with something.

Sometimes, He bestows knowledge by
teaching me a lesson and sometimes
He gives me a gift.

I prefer the Gift.

s.hukr

Noor upon Noor

Love people in such a way that your love is
pure. It is not a desperate or needy type of
love, nor does your love vary by how much
someone loves you back.

Love people purely for the sake of Allah and
watch how your love (with time)
travels to their hearts.

s.hukr

Noor upon Noor

To all my Kings:

Make so much money but don't tell a soul.
Win so many hearts but don't tell a soul.
You don't need to tell people anything.

Silence is also an answer because your actions
will speak louder than words ever would.

s.hukr

Noor upon Noor

If you make my heart smile,
perhaps ill melt your heart
until it flows like honey.

s.hukr

Noor upon Noor

I don't like it when people praise me.

I much rather they spend time thanking
Allah. Praising me will just feed my ego
and I want to stay humble.

Thank Allah instead. For He is
the one who guided me to you.

s.hukr

Noor upon Noor

I've never actually had a celebrity crush
because I can't crush on someone based
solely off their looks, I just don't find people
attractive like that.

But a woman who has the ability to catch
my attention with her mindset and her
personality, has probably already
won my heart.

s.hukr

Noor upon Noor

"God has gifted every woman the
patience of 10 men and during
pregnancy she gains the ability
of 10 more men."

s.hukr

Noor upon Noor

Sometimes,

I wanna go to the house of Allah.
Forget about everything and focus
on what really matters.

I'm not tired of this world,
I'm just tired of the people
of this world.

Because when I spend time with
people of the Quran, I feel like I'm
amongst people of Paradise.

Are you from the people
of the Quran...?

s.hukr

Noor upon Noor

As soon as you reach the age of adulthood,
you cannot be friends with the opposite
gender outside your immediate family, at least
not how the west portrays it.

This is to protect each other from
broken hearts, Zina, and immortality.

It doesn't mean you cannot communicate or
socialise with each other, but it must be within
the limits set by Allah.

With Haya, respect and in public light.

Only talk if there is something that needs to be
discussed or there is genuine purpose behind
it. Refrain from mingling with the opposite
gender without genuine purpose.

There is wisdom behind it.

s.hukr

Noor upon Noor

I am not a teacher to
teach you anything.

God has gifted you a
mind, hands and feet.

Use them as best as you
can and when you get
lost, raise your hands
and talk to God.

And in your heart let
there be hope, because
God always responds.

s.hukr

Noor upon Noor

Kind loving words makes a woman's
heart move but ever wondered what
makes a man's heart move?

s.hukr

Noor upon Noor

I don't want your money,
your time is more valuable.

I don't want your gifts,
your Dua is more valuable.

I don't want your eyes,
I only want passage to
your heart.

So I can win it
every day.

s.hukr

Noor upon Noor

Have you ever met a soul so sweet
that whenever you see them your
heart smiles?

Nothing else matters when you are
in the presence of someone
who is loved by God.

s.hukr

Noor upon Noor

If you are a true Soldier of Allah,
nothing will scare you, not even death.

Because you live and die purely
for the sake of Allah.

s.hukr

Noor upon Noor

There is a hidden world of
Kings and Queens and Lovers.

People that live up to their gifts,
they live their best lives by pushing
themselves towards Greatness.

I always admire such people because
this life is not kind to them.

s.hukr

Noor upon Noor

A man works all his life for what?
To acquire wealth for himself?

Nah, he works hard not for himself but for
others. His shoulders are heavy with the
responsibility to provide, protect and lead a
generation of people.

Yet some men come to house not a home, a
witch not a wife, hardship not ease. And
people wonder why he left for the milk
and never came back.

s.hukr

Noor upon Noor

Turn your calamities into festivities
and your faith into a weapon.

Be so close to God,
that if you wish a thing,
He always grants it to you
or gives you something better.

s.hukr

Noor upon Noor

There was once a King. Nobody
knew his name and he didn't care.

When I asked him why? He told
me that God knew who he was
and that was enough for him.

s.hukr

Noor upon Noor

You live near the sea and
I live near the mountains.

You watch the sunsets
while I watch the sunrise.

You live far away but one
day we shall meet.

I will read your eyes and
forget about the sky.

You will hold my hand
and forget about the moon.

s.hukr

Noor upon Noor

As long as we stay divided
under nationalities created
by the west. We will suffer.

Only when we choose to
unite under God's book.
Only then will we triumph.

s.hukr

Noor upon Noor

Please don't disturb my peace.
If you have something to say
don't.

Tell God instead.

s.hukr

Noor upon Noor

I miss the old days when life
was simple and love was plentiful.

Common sense was common and
people knew in their heart what was
right and what was wrong.

Now... it only gets worse as time passes.

s.hukr

Noor upon Noor

It is not the dress that I find attractive.

It is your modesty. It's not the makeup that makes me smile, it's the Noor glowing from within you.

I wish you understood this...

s.hukr

Noor upon Noor

Be the soul that follows the righteous path
that isn't easy, but it is the most rewarding.

s.hukr

Noor upon Noor

I appreciate kindness.

I appreciate those who ask me if I'm okay.

I appreciate every person in my life who has
tried to brighten my day and succeeded.

s.hukr

Noor upon Noor

A true Queen never claims to be a Queen
and a true King never claims to be a King.

Don't tell people how good you are or
what you do, don't go outside your way
to show off your wealth, your status and
whatever Allah has blessed you with.

Stay hidden, for gems are meant to be
hidden in plain sight.

s.hukr

Noor upon Noor

I think marriage is a beautiful bond that
unites two people, two different families,
two different bloodlines and instils
love between them.

It a way to unite and strengthen this ummah.

Love has no language boundaries.
Love doesn't discriminate.
Love doesn't care how rich or poor you are.

True love overcomes many obstacles,
but you must be willing to **sacrifice**.

s.hukr

Noor upon Noor

The mosque is free of charge
but most of the time it's empty.

The clubs and shisha lounges,
places of sin, are paid but mostly full.

It's free to earn Jannah and
expensive to earn Hell.

s.hukr

Noor upon Noor

There is no wealth like intelligence,
no poverty like ignorance and
no inheritance like good manners.

s.hukr

How to impress any Woman:
1. Maintain a strong connection with Allah
2. Knows how to cook & dress well
3. Be great with children
4. Be Mentally and physically fit
5. Have good speech
6. Never lie
7. Have Haya
8. Have ambitions & goals
9. Be protective but not insecure
10. Knowledgeable in Deen & Dunya

s.hukr

How to impress any Man:
1. Be God Conscious
2. Not be a Feminist
3. Be emotionally intelligent
4. Be great with children
5. Not be clingy or insecure
6. Knowledgeable in Deen
7. Obedient
8. Hijab & Haya
9. Is playful
10. Makes great food

s.hukr

Noor upon Noor

Women desire 2 main things,
one is respect, the other is love.

If you don't love her, she won't
leave you but if you don't respect her.

She will definitely leave you.

s.hukr

Noor upon Noor

Salam,

I know this might be random,
but I hope you have an amazing
day full of blessings and that Allah
guides your beautiful soul towards
Paradise.

Don't let the temporary enjoyments
of this world get to you because I
would really like to meet you in
Paradise one day.

s.hukr

Noor upon Noor

Can we normalise saying السلام عليكم to other
Muslims instead of Hey or Hello

Make it so normalised that even non-Muslims
say Salam instead of Hello.

s.hukr

Noor upon Noor

I firmly believe that every person has a gift
from Allah. Some are blessed with creativity
and some with an analytical mindset, some are
naturally lucky, and some are talented in other
areas.

But each and every one of us is born with a
potential for greatness deep inside us. It is very
sad that many of us spend our whole life
unable to reach our true potential and are
withered away by meaningless worldly
pursuits.

s.hukr

Noor upon Noor

Happiness was asked:

"Where do you live?"

It replied: "In the hearts of those content with Allah's decree."

s.hukr

Noor upon Noor

A woman who loves and supports
you when you have nothing, she
deserves everything and more.

s.hukr

Noor upon Noor

The same way you go to the gym
to build up physical health is the same
way you go to the library to
build up mental health.

These days you don't even
need a library, almost everything
can be accessed from a few taps
on your phone.

For how long will you stay miserable
because of your lack of awareness.

Allah doesn't burden a soul more
than he can bare, but sometimes
you burden yourself more than you
can bare by not following Islam to
the best of your ability.

s.hukr

Noor upon Noor

Be careful of who
you call your friend.

Their influence will rub off on
you over time. If you accompany
yourself with wrongdoers, your
likelihood of becoming like them
increases exponentially.

s.hukr

Prophet ﷺ said: "A person is on the religion of his companions. Therefore, let every one of you carefully consider the company he keeps."

- Tirmidhi

Noor upon Noor

Some people chase
success but I never did.

I never wanted to be rich,
famous or anything.

I liked my simple lifestyle.
However, success was chasing
me while I was chasing Allah.

My life changed once I
understood the beauty
behind God's words.

s.hukr

Noor upon Noor

Being humble, wise and sincere.
Now that's attractive.

s.hukr

Noor upon Noor

As a man, you are the leader, the breadwinner, the one in charge and the one with responsibility. The one accountable for your family.

Your job isn't to lead according to what your wife says or what your father says, their job is to advice you as best as they can, not to control you or to make decisions for you. Allah appointed you to make the final decision according to the principles & values of Islam.

Your job isn't just to earn Rizq for your family, you must also be present in the upbringing of your children, ensuring the next generation continues to excel in Deen and Dunya. Your children will be a reflection of you, so you must push yourself towards greatness. You will be an example for your children.

You must spend time and energy on your marriage, with your wife, invest in your marriage so it doesn't crumble into heart break. It's not about money, it's about time, communication and sacrifices. Establish a deep understanding with her and help her, support her, be there for her. She is your wife. The mother of your children.

s.hukr

Noor upon Noor

Don't be that man that is cursed
by Allah because he neglected his
responsibility upon his wife, his
family, and his Deen.

Pleasing people is an impossible
task. Instead, spend your energy
pleasing the almighty and watch
how your life changes overnight.

s.hukr

Noor upon Noor

Towards the end of every year,
I like to reflect upon my life.
Do a recap of what happened
and what didn't.

Ponder about the new people
I met and people who have left me.
Go over significant events that have
lead me to the path I am on today.

And check if I have achieved the goals
I have set for myself or did my goals change?
Am I getting to where I want to be?

I keep asking myself questions to measure and
determine my progress. Because if I die
tomorrow, I want to have lived a life that I
would be happy to die upon.

s.hukr

Noor upon Noor

Why do you think that a good heart is
someone who doesn't pray?

A heart without hijab
and a heart who overthinks?

A heart without the remembrance of Allah,
how can it be good?

Tell me!

That's not a good heart, that's a heart
filled with doubts, fears and darkness.

Why do you allow Shaytan to brainwash
you into thinking that your heart is good
when half the time you feel empty inside?

Hopefully, there might be some light in
you, so use that light and recognise
the true condition of your heart so that
you can do something about it.

s.hukr

Noor upon Noor

A good heart has peace within,
tranquillity and love pouring
down like a spring.

A good heart doesn't neglect or disobey
Allah. A good heart is someone who
lives life according to true nature of Islam.

Living a lifestyle dictated by God.

s.hukr

Noor upon Noor

You can't be successful in Deen
without Dunya. Neither can you
be successful in Dunya without Deen.

You need both as a Muslim.

A True Muslim is someone who
strives for the best in worldly matters
while establishing himself firm in faith.

Faith is a component of your character, your
ethics, your principles and morality. It is what
makes you different from non-Muslims but
also the reason that excels you in Dunya.
Because you are blessed by Allah for being a
real Muslim.

s.hukr

Noor upon Noor

Deen isn't just about praying 5 times, it is so much more than that. It is how to live life in this Dunya.

Deen & Dunya go hand in hand
and a True Muslim is a master of both.

s.hukr

Noor upon Noor

Be happy in whatever stage of life
you are. Accept your reality but also
try your absolute best.

Be grateful for everything and
enjoy whatever life brings your way.

Last I checked, a Muslim doesn't stress
over worldly things, we stress over the
matters of the hereafter.

s.hukr

Noor upon Noor

If you are rich, spend
time with the poor.

If you are righteous, spend
time with those who are not.

If you are young, spend
time with the old.

If you were raised in the west,
spend time in the east.

You won't understand the other
side of life until you go exploring.

s.hukr

Noor upon Noor

People love to blame their mistakes and
flaws on everything other than themselves.

If there is a will, there is a way.

s.hukr

Noor upon Noor

I'm convinced that age doesn't matter,
it's your ability to adapt to different
people of different ages. Sometimes
you need more patience and sometimes
you need more love.

Age is just a measurement of how long
you have lived. It doesn't define your
status or character or anything else
important. Don't give it so much weight.

s.hukr

Noor upon Noor

Your diet has a huge role to play
on your body's health and well-being.

It affects your mood, your ability
to stay active, your behaviour, your
skin, your mental health.

"If you eat like an animal then
you become an animal"

Modern day sickness such as
high blood pressure, heart attack,
cancer etc are partly due to one's diet.

So eat that which is good for
you, and fast from time to time.

That is better than to be
stuck in hospital.

s.hukr

Noor upon Noor

The Root of all diseases is within our heart.
The love and attachment to this materialistic
world stems from our heart.

We know this world is temporary, yet we
find it so hard to disengage from it.

May the Almighty guide our hearts into
desiring what is lasting - the Hereafter.

Remember, the life of this world
is merely enjoyment of delusion.

s.hukr

Noor upon Noor

Some people are so precious.

They deserve more than your heart.
They deserve your Duas at Tahajjud.

s.hukr

Noor upon Noor

Many of you have yet to win
the war inside of you.

For as long as you allow overthinking,
worries, doubts, fears, and insecurities
to plague your heart and mind.

You will remain weak in my perception.

s.hukr

Noor upon Noor

Idk who needs to hear this but stop developing feelings for people outside of marriage.

Takes max 2 weeks to get to know someone and 1 week to get married, not 8 months and then I'll think about out.

or 5 months and I'm heartbroken and it's not my fault. You attract and repel people based on who you are, not who they are.

s.hukr

Noor upon Noor

Are you slave of money?

Are you a slave of the school system?

Are you a slave of your ego?

Are you a slave of what people
think about you?

Are you a slave of materialistic desires?

Are you a slave of your emotions?

Are you a slave of another human?

Are you a slave of things other than Allah?

If you said **Yes** to any of them,
you are committing shirk.

s.hukr

Noor upon Noor

Prioritise people over worldly things.
It might be a Dua that saves you from
hell fire.

s.hukr

Noor upon Noor

I am at peace because I know that Allah
greatest work happens in the most
impossible situations.

s.hukr

Noor upon Noor

Please don't criticise someone in front of everyone. Make that conversation private.

Hide sins, hide mistakes, don't expose them.

s.hukr

Noor upon Noor

I talk about love and people
assume I'm in love.

I talk about Islam and people
assume I'm a sheikh.

I talk about money and
people assume I'm rich.

I talk about women and people
assume I'm misogynistic.

I talk about knowledge and
people assume I'm smart.

Why can't I be free to talk about anything without
you declaring your assumption about me?

You don't even know me.
I never asked and I don't wanna know.
I don't care. Keep it yourself.

God knows who I am and
that's all that matters.

s.hukr

Noor upon Noor

Some people will never change,
no matter how much you care.

s.hukr

Noor upon Noor

Unfortunately, we live in a world where
the bare minimum is treated like gold.

s.hukr

Noor upon Noor

Thank you for reading this book.

I hope that you enjoyed it and found some benefit from my words.

May Allah always have mercy on you and guide you towards the straight path. **Ameen.**

Sincerely,
s.hukr

P.S If you love this book, please promote them and share it with others and maybe you'll earn a good deed and guide someone towards Jannah!

P.S.S If you loved this book, you should checkout my other books.

fajrnoor.com.au

S.hukr Books

1. Fajr and Noor

2. Through His Eyes

3. Noor upon Noor

4. Slice of Paradise